McCall Collection of Modern Art

Utrillo and the Painters of Montmartre

Published by Fratelli Fabbri Editori,
Publishers, Milan, Italy, and

The McCall Publishing Company
New York, New York

Utrillo's Montmartre

Many artists have found subjects worthy of their talents in such cities as Venice, London, Toledo, New York, and Paris. But no artist ever produced so detailed a portrait of a city as Maurice Utrillo did of Montmartre—that hill north of the Seine that was the original artists' quarter of Paris. Montmartre was Utrillo's obsession. It was his lifelong and almost exclusive subject in his paintings. There was scarcely a street, an alley, a wall, a church, or the facade of a house in Montmartre that he did not paint at least once. Many views he painted several times—a house seen from one angle and then from another, a street from one direction and then from another, a square at one season of the year and then at another. Together his paintings make a composite portrait that is unique in art.

This portrait is not, however, what we would expect of a place that has long been considered the gayest quarter of the gayest city in the world. The very name of Montmartre brings to mind the Bohemian life, vivid, colorful, convivial, amoral, alcoholic, and boisterous. But Utrillo's Montmartre is the antithesis of this. Its pervasive mood is one of melancholy and loneliness. Its streets and narrow byways are sad, its sky is leaden. Its windows are shuttered and blind. Few people inhabit it, and they are almost invariably walking away from the viewer, isolating him from human companionship. No sound breaks the stillness. No bird flies through the overcast sky, no air rustles the sparse leaves. The few pedestrians move noiselessly, like ghosts, or else are frozen into immobility as if caught by some dark enchantment.

PISSARRO *The Boulevard Montmartre on a Winter Morning* (65 x 81 cm) New York, Metropolitan Museum

Such a portrait is obviously a double one. It presents the physical features of Montmartre, but it is the spiritual portrait of Utrillo. And his is a tragic spirit, in accord with a life that was almost unrelievedly tragic.

Suzanne Valadon

But to understand Utrillo and his work, we must first become acquainted with his mother and the facts of his birth. Marie-Clémentine Valadon was a handsome country girl from the vicinity of Limoges, the daughter of a washerwoman and an unknown father. Impelled by a youthful lust for life, she came to Paris at the age of fourteen and made her living in any way she could. She must have been a girl of considerable strength as well as spirit. She worked as a waitress and barmaid, vegetable seller, nursemaid, and circus acrobat. After she had been in Paris for a year, she changed her name to Suzanne and became an artists' model. She posed for Puvis de Chavannes, Renoir, and Toulouse-Lautrec (Plate 51), and she won the friendship of irascible old Degas, who called her "the terrible little Marie" and encouraged her in her drawing.

At sixteen Suzanne Valadon became pregnant and gave birth to a son whom she named Maurice. Who the boy's father was has never been determined. Possibly she did not know herself. Various opinions have been expressed by people who were acquainted with her. Some said that Puvis de Chavannes was the father; others named Boissy, a kind of vagabond art student of Montmartre who was notorious; still others found an amazing resemblance between Maurice's features and those of Miguel Utrillo, a Spanish journalist who legally recognized him in 1891 in order to give him a name. In any case Maurice's male parent was not a father, but merely the cause of his existence. And his mother, so young and so preoccupied with her own affairs, had little time for her accidental and unwanted encumbrance. She went her vagabond way as a model. Among her casual lovers were Toulouse-Lautrec and the composer Erik Satie, who was her neighbor in rue Cortot.

Utrillo's own view of his mother and his presentation of the facts of his birth are interesting—and very moving—in their divergence from reality. He opens his memoirs thus:

"Well, dear reader, one must begin at the beginning. I was born in Paris, in

3

the rue du Poteau, on 25 December, Christmas Day, in the year of grace, 1882. My mother, a saintly woman, whom in the depths of my heart I bless and revere as a goddess, a sublime example of goodness, rectitude, charity, unselfishness, intelligence, courage, and devotion, a woman apart, brought me up in a consistently strict code of morals, right, and duty."

The most obvious error in this opening paragraph is the date Utrillo gives for his birth. Evidently he found Christmas Day a more interesting date of birth than the day recorded on his birth certificate, which was December 26. He mistook the year also, though that error was probably unintentional. He was born a year later than he said, in 1883.

As for his description of his mother, although it manifests a very honest and very touching devotion, almost no one would consider it realistic. On the contrary, it seems, at first reading, so far removed from reality as to appear ludicrous. But that opinion may be softened by a second reading of Utrillo's words. After all, who is to say what constitutes saintliness? Just as the Montmartre that Utrillo painted was as true and honest a record as he was capable of making, so his description of his mother was truth as he felt it.

The care of the child, Maurice, was put in the hands of Grand'mère Coulon, a "pretend" grandmother who was well-intentioned but permissive and who let him do as he pleased rather than risk his tantrums. "He is a darling," she would say, "but I wonder what he has in his blood. Sometimes he frightens me."

Apparently what he had in his blood was rebellion. He had no father and, for the moment, no mother but Grand'mère Coulon, and he must have felt some difference from other children. He was a high-strung, frequently savage child, who rarely smiled and never laughed. His words were as few as his smiles, and he confided his troubles to no one. He rebelled against authority from whatever quarter. At first the only authority, lax though it was, was from Grand'mère Coulon. Later objects of his rebellion were his stepfather, his teachers, his employers, and policemen.

Utrillo's Youth in Montmagny and Paris

When he was ten years old, his mother began an affair with a prosperous business man, Moussis, whom she married three years later. The family moved into a large house at Butte-Pinson in Montmagny, six miles north of Paris, and there, materially at least, life was easier for Maurice and his mother.

At first he went as a day student to a private boarding school in Montmagny. He was a thin boy, with delicate, rather bony features and long, pale hands, and he was the victim of brutality for his schoolmates, the sons of wealthy, local manufacturers. Often his white beret served as their football. Later Moussis sent him to a school in Paris to which he commuted by train. He was a poor student in most of his classes, but he excelled in mathematics and won a prize in calculus three times. In art his grade was "very poor." Until it clouded over, his mind was quick and alert, but he had no perseverance and never received his diploma.

His daily trips to and from school necessitated some waiting in the railroad station. It may have been in the station bars that he discovered the solace of alcohol. Perhaps the wagoners with whom he occasionally returned home found it amusing to introduce him to the effects of absinthe. Given his temperament, he would have resorted to drink sooner or later. As it happened, he became a child drunkard. Evening after evening he returned late from school in stages of intoxication varying from mild euphoria to stupefaction.

His stepfather withdrew him from school and found him employment in a bank. With his natural aptitude for figures he might have done well, but his hatred of authority showed itself again, and he was fired for impertinence.

He drank more and more. He threatened to throw himself from his bedroom window if his bottle was taken from him. By the time he was eighteen he was a confirmed alcoholic, and his seizures had become so violent that he was sent to the sanatorium of St. Anne for two months' treatment.

He was released as a cured patient, but the cure was only temporary. Genuinely alarmed at last, his mother did her best to interest him in art as therapy. It was not easy, since he had not the slightest natural desire to paint. Art was forced on him. "Maurice, you *must* not sit there dreaming. Do something! Go and paint!" And patiently, to please his mother, he would sit at the window and copy onto cardboard his view of the street below. He had innate talent, but he had absolutely no inclination. If it had not been for his devotion to his mother, who forced it, his talent would probably never have appeared.

His friend Quizet also helped interest him in painting. Like Utrillo, Quizet painted only Paris, but in a very different style (Plates 49 and 27). The two worked together in complete silence, which was evidently an important condition of their painting as well as of their friendship. Mental solitude was always Utrillo's refuge whether he was alone or in company.

It has long been said that Utrillo's mother arranged his palette for him with only five colors: zinc white, two chrome yellows, vermilion, and crimson lake. This may, perhaps, have been true in the very beginning of his painting career; no one can either prove or disprove it, since all of Utrillo's earliest paintings have disappeared. It is certainly not true of the paintings that remain, for even the earliest of these, from 1903 and 1904, include umbers and black, as well as a great variety of blues and greens.

The unwilling painter discovered one day that an unexpected benefit might be reaped from his work. The paintings on cardboard could occasionally be exchanged in a bistro for a glass or two of red wine. Edmond Heuzé, who knew Utrillo for many years, said that he would paint wherever he was offered a glass of wine, and he would abandon his work on the spot. "Sometimes Suzanne Valadon would ask the neighborhood boys, 'Have you seen Maurice?' 'Yes,' they would say, 'he was in the rue Norvins a minute ago.' 'Go and see if he has left a painting there.' And the boys would bring back a canvas as they might have brought in eggs from the henhouse."

William Blake said that artists paint better when they are drunk. Perhaps it was so with Utrillo. But more likely he was, as his mother said, reasonably sober while painting, and promised himself the alcoholic reward only when he finished his work at the end of the afternoon. Then he would go from bar to bar through the Butte, ending perhaps in Place Pigalle, where Heuzé saw him once "with his arms outstretched like a Christ on the cross, planted in the path of an autobus, forcing the conductor to get out and beat him up to get him out of the way."

He seemed purposely to attract persecution, and when he was drunk he was dominated by a destructive force that frightened even himself. He vented his rage particularly on glass; mirrors and the shop windows in which he saw his face reflected, or the small glass windows of fire alarm boxes he smashed with fury, continuing to strike them even as the lights of the police van were appearing around the corner of the street. He insulted pregnant women, for whom he had a special aversion. He picked up bar companions who would later beat him and leave him unconscious in the gutter. Night after night he would be returned to his home with his face swollen and bleeding, his clothing muddied and torn.

A friend described him as he appeared at such a time, "I have seen him fall from his seat onto the floor of La Belle Gabrielle," wrote Francis Carco. "I have seen him rush out, trying to escape from the police, dashing himself against the walls in the midnight-black streets."

Many times his mother was forced to go to the police station in rue Lambert or rue Clignancourt to claim him. He was once sent to a special prison infirmary for "having beaten without cause Madame François, of 15 rue St. Vincent, striking her repeatedly across the back with a pot, and for having broken the glass in the fire alarm box in rue du Mont-Cenis." The police report added that Utrillo apparently "was not in full possession of his faculties."

Surely no artist was ever physically mistreated to such an extent as was Utrillo. He was beaten in police stations, occasionally beaten at home by his mother's lovers, beaten in bars by chance acquaintances, mistreated in clinics and prison hospitals and hospitals for the insane. Despair was perhaps the cause of his persecution as it was of his self-abasement, his humiliation, his debauches of alcohol, his laziness, and his general indifference. Despair made him utterly vulnerable, as a child is vulnerable.

The only place where he felt truly at home was in the street. In the words of Aristide Bruant's song, "T'es dans la rue, va, t'es chez toi!" ("There, you're in the street, you're at home!") And the streets that were his home were those of Montmartre. He knew every angle of them, every twisting lane and hidden alley. Repelled by humanity, his love turned to inanimate things, to pavements, windows, fences, and especially to walls.

Utrillo's Paintings

The earliest pictures that remain with us are those dating from 1903. This early period and the "white period" that followed it are generally considered to be his best. Like his life, his art evolved in reverse. His early art is, if not sophisticated, certainly not in the least primitive. It is technically very "painterly."

The brushstrokes are free and fluid, the paint is applied thickly and handled easily. The style borders on virtuosity. Outlines are absorbed into the forms. The influence of Impressionism is obvious, particularly of Sisley, whom Utrillo much admired.

Over the years Utrillo's art progressed backward. It became almost primitive, sometimes childlike, with a strange—and appealing—quality of innocence that is lacking in his earlier pictures. It loses its painterly quality. The dry, tight surfaces of his later canvases come to resemble tempera more than oil paint. Outline, which is absent from his early period, becomes prominent.

The years from 1903 to about 1910 constitute his Montmagny period, although he painted in Montmartre as well as in the Butte-Pinson (Plates 1 and 4), for he and his mother had returned to Montmartre, to rue Cortot, even before her break with Moussis in 1909. Utrillo painted diligently. His work was always honest and conscientious and spontaneous. The schoolboy ability that he had shown in mathematics expressed itself in his love of the architectural geometry of buildings, in perspective and in deep space. He was not a two-dimensional painter. He would not have agreed with Cézanne about the inviolability of the picture plane and the importance of "flattening" perspective. Montmartre was a high place, as was the Butte-Pinson. Whether he looked out over Paris from the square of St. Pierre or up or down the steep and narrow streets, space opened out before him. With Paolo Uccello he seems to be exclaiming, "What a marvel this perspective is!" And, perhaps, there may be a yearning for escape in his great love of space.

The *Square St. Pierre, Montmartre* (Plate 3) is a good example of this feeling for space as well as of the free painting style and dark but bright colors of his Montmagny period. Windows are an obsession with him, as can be seen by comparing this painting with a similar one by Van Gogh, *View of Paris from Montmartre* (Plate 47).

The motif of deep space in a street scene, as the street twists upward or downward into the distance, occurs again and again. An example from the Montmagny period is *Rue Lepic and the Moulin de la Galette* (Plate 2). The rue Lepic was built by Napoleon III as a carriage road up the slope of the hill, which explains its frequent changes of direction. It is one of the most meandering of Paris streets. Vincent Van Gogh once lived with his brother Theo at 54 rue Lepic.

Such small bits of history or legend are attached to almost all of Utrillo's paintings. It could scarcely be otherwise, as the history of Montmartre predates the arrival of the Romans by many years. The Church of Sacré-Coeur (Plate 36), which Zola called "this monument of absurdity and affront" and which has been more recently and more precisely described as "a monstrous vanilla sun-

8

dae," rises on the site of the sacrificial groves of the Parisii, a Gallic tribe who lived on the swampy island in the middle of the Seine that is now the heart of Paris. Beneath Sacré-Coeur were the gypsum quarries that, from the fourteenth century, produced so much plaster of paris.

Probably the most remarkable event ever to take place in Montmartre occurred in 250 A.D. Paris was then a Roman settlement called Lutetia, perhaps from the Latin word for muddy or miry. In that year Dionysius came from Rome to Lutetia to evangelize and to become the town's first bishop. With him came two other priests, Rusticus and Eleutherius. Dionysius, acting according to his evangelical duty, desecrated the temple of Mars, which then occupied approximately the site of the Moulin de la Galette (Plates 30 and 45). For this crime the Roman governor had the three priests beheaded. An old chronicle relates the miracle that then took place, "And anone the body of Saynte Denys reysed himself up and bare his hede betwene his armes." Carrying his head, Dionysius walked more than two miles to the north, until he reached the spot where he wished his chapel to be raised, and there he found a Christian convert to bury him and his friends. As Saint Denis he is now the patron saint of France, and the great Basilica of Saint-Denis (Plate 7) marks his resting place. It is from this event that Montmartre takes its name, Mons Martyrum, the hill of the martyrs.

Utrillo's painting of the Basilica of Saint-Denis is a remarkably beautiful one. The architectural forms are reduced to a geometric simplicity that is almost abstract, and the colors are jewel-like. The intricacy of Gothic detail is only suggested. Utrillo had a very particular feeling for churches, and his paintings of cathedrals and churches have a very important place in his work. "His most spectacular paintings," Vlaminck wrote, "are perhaps certain cathedrals that contain a true mystic power. When Utrillo paints the imposing bulk of a basilica, or the pointed spire of a village chapel, he unconsciously expresses the love that man feels toward God."

The Cathedral (Plate 22), like the painting of Saint-Denis, is almost abstract. It is a simple but very massive and powerful composition of blocks, "the portrait of a giant in stone." Even when he painted a small church, which in reality is not at all imposing, Utrillo imbues it with dignity and importance, as in *The Church of Notre-Dame de Clignancourt* (Plate 21).

One of the streets that Utrillo painted many times is the rue du Mont-Cenis (Plates 12, 24, 35). At No. 12 of this street are studios that at various times were occupied by Renoir, Gauguin, Van Gogh, and Dufy, as well as by Suzanne Valadon and Utrillo. The rue du Mont-Cenis was formerly the only road leading from Montmartre to the north, and was the route taken by Saint Denis after losing his head. During the Middle Ages his martyrdom was celebrated every seven years with a procession from the Basilica of Saint-Denis to the Abbey of Montmartre. Four monks in red led the procession, bearing the head of the saint.

The house of Berlioz and the hunting lodge of Henry IV were at the junction of rue du Mont-Cenis and rue Saint-Vincent; compare Corot's painting of the latter (Plate 46) with Utrillo's (Plate 32). These subjects Utrillo also painted repeatedly. Berlioz lived in the small white house from 1834 to 1837, not very happily, with his English wife. Henry IV took occasional shelter, more pleasurably we presume, with his mistress, Gabrielle d'Estrées, in the house with the thatched roof.

Bars and bistros were also favorite subjects. *A la Belle Gabrielle* — perhaps named after Gabrielle d'Estrées — (Plate 23) was one of the bars most frequented by Utrillo. Marie Vizier was, along with Gay, the proprietor of the cafe Casse-Croute and among Utrillo's warmest friends. They frequently extended their hospitality to him without charge, giving him a room in which to work as well as to sleep. They gave him money when he was in greatest need, and occasionally they sold his paintings. It was at Gay's that he wrote his naive and touching memoirs, which have never been published.

Another favorite cafe was Le Lapin Agile (Plates 5 and 37), also frequented by Picasso and Max Jacob. With its prominent white fence it is one of the best-known landmarks of Montmartre. The name of the Lively Rabbit is due to the fact that an artist named A. Gill painted the picture of the rabbit over the front door.

Stylistic Changes

Around 1910, during his "white period," a change of style became apparent in Utrillo's work. The Impressionist influence disappears entirely. His palette is lightened. His predominant whites are vibrant with color in subtle and delicate shades and are contrasted with deep browns and black. Occasionally he mixed plaster of paris with his paint in order to achieve the effect he wanted of walls that are ancient, lichen-encrusted, peeling and crumbling and stained with a mixture of filth and whitewash.

Louis Libaude

Until this time a number of junk dealers and the frame maker Anzoli had been the only dealers in Utrillo's pictures. But about 1909 or 1910, Louis Libaude, a writer who had become an art dealer, became interested in Utrillo's work. Libaude exploited him, paying him three hundred francs a month for his entire output, but at the same time credit must be given to Libaude for discovering him and for preserving his early paintings in the Impressionist style.

It was in Libaude's shop that Elie Faure and Octave Mirbeau "discovered" Utrillo. It was Libaude who, in 1913, organized the first exhibition of Utrillo's work at the Blot Gallery. Thirty-one paintings were exhibited, of which only two were sold. In his introduction to the catalogue Libaude wrote, "Maurice Utrillo is the painter of Montmartre. He renders with acute sensitivity the sad charm of this little provincial town, isolated on the summit of Paris. He excels in painting the cracked walls of the old houses. The smallest, meanest facade takes on in his paintings an extraordinary intensity of color and life. He loves the morose steeples of old churches, the deserted streets of the gloomy suburbs …their sickly sky, their resigned houses."

In 1912, after an attack of delirium tremens, Utrillo was sent to a nursing home in Sannois, not far from Montmartre, where he remained for several months. Such sojourns, increasingly frequent, were invariably followed by relapses. Heuzé recalls seeing Utrillo depart for one of his clinical stays, "dressed all in black, with a small suitcase hung from a rope about his neck, with his paint box at his side and a sketch pad under his right arm."

In 1914 he was back at Sannois. In 1916 he was put into a hospital for the insane in Villejuif. Two years later, in 1918, he was in still another clinic, in Aulnay-sous-Bois, from which he escaped and sought refuge with his friend Gay of the Cafe Casse-Croute. He signed a promise to Gay, dated September 6, not to go out of his room before the end of the month, but he disappeared a few days later. That same year he voluntarily committed himself to the clinic in Picpus, where his expenses were paid by the generous Polish art dealer

Leopold Zborowski, who had helped Modigliani and Soutine. The following year Utrillo was again in Picpus.

He continued to produce paintings in great numbers. After 1916 other changes are apparent in his style. The colors are brighter but also cruder than in the "white period," and there is more emphasis on outline. The paintings are vivid but lack the depth and power of the earlier works. Utrillo is more concerned with detail, especially printed signs, and sometimes he writes his own comments or explanations at the bottom of his paintings. The childish element in his art becomes more pronounced. This had been evident as early as 1912, in his *Utrillo's Arrest at Montmartre* (Plate 16), and reappeared spasmodically, becoming a constant characteristic of his late work. But childishness in art is not necessarily a bad thing. It may manifest itself as a freshness of vision, a kind of innocence, and a feeling of regeneration and renewal.

An interesting but minor change in his art is noticeable in his manner of drawing women. After about 1920 or 1922 begins the style that critics call the period of the *"gros derrières,"* the big behinds (Plate 34). Utrillo had always been repelled and frightened by women, and this new manner may have been an indication of sexual frustration. He draws women with enormous buttocks and with an exaggerated sexuality, as if they were primitive fertility idols. They are always drawn from the back, moving away from him. "Art is a means of satisfying those desires that one cannot exercise," Utrillo once said.

He was excluded not merely from the society of women but from all society. Only inanimate objects held any attraction for him. In his paintings trees, animals, and people are anonymous. They have no vitality, no significance. His world is purely architectural. Only houses and walls have individuality.

"There are souls hidden away in these secretive houses," he wrote to his mother. But he was unable to see inside the houses. Whatever souls were there were strangers to him. When he attempted to paint an interior, as in his sketch for the first act of *Louise* (Plate 40), his room exudes an emptiness beyond that of any empty stage in the world. An empty room, like a bare stage, can be alive with a feeling of expectancy, of people or actors soon to enter and live or enact their lives in it. But Utrillo's room awaits no one. Its doors do not open, they are merely painted on the wall. In fact, if the door next to the large window should, miraculously, open, only a bird could possibly enter. And in another sketch for *Louise* (Plate 41), we notice something curious about the window. Utrillo is so accustomed to his exclusion, to viewing the world from the outside, that he has painted the white curtains on the outside of the windows, as he would see them from the street.

Exhibitions of Utrillo's Works

An exhibition in 1919 at the Galerie Lepoultre was such a success that when he was next shut up in a psychiatric clinic his keepers exploited him. He was given wine and painting materials, and his paintings were confiscated. When the truth of his treatment began to leak out and a scandal threatened, he was permitted to "escape."

After 1923, the date of his first truly important and highly successful exhibit at the Bernheim-Jeune Gallery, Utrillo was given a contract with three galleries and an assured income of one million francs a year. His mother's second husband, an artist named André Utter, took charge of his affairs, as Utrillo had become completely incompetent to manage his own life. Following an attempted suicide in 1924, he lived with his mother and Utter, a virtual prisoner in the sumptuous house that his art had provided, the Chateau Saint-Bernard not far from Lyon. Between his attacks he worked, prayed, looked through his souvenirs, and played with his electric train.

Lucie Valore

In order to assure his protection and care after her death, Suzanne Valadon arranged the marriage of her son and Lucie Valore, a former actress and the widow of a Belgian banker. Utrillo and Lucie moved to Le Vesinet, to a villa called the "good Lucie." There he continued to paint, rather like a small boy doing his homework, sometimes working from memory and sometimes from postcards. Painting from postcards was not new to him. Often in the past he had preferred such a method to working directly from his subject in the street, where he risked encounters with street urchins and passersby. His mother said of him, "So many painters just turn out picture postcards when confronted by nature, but my son uses postcards to make masterpieces."

13

Lucie continued to watch over him after his mother's death. She diluted his wine with water, rebottled and resealed it. She called him her "jewel-husband," and kept him on his good behavior and saw that he worked at his painting every day. His art, perhaps not surprisingly, became more mechanical and more concise. It may be that his natural genius required physical suffering and mental anguish in order to thrive, and that it faded in luxurious and peaceful captivity. The quality of innocence remained, however, in his painting as in his life. It was as if a guardian angel bearing a chalice of red wine watched over him always, through all the vicissitudes of his life, keeping him free from any inner depravity or stain.

"One can try to analyze Utrillo," Derain said, "but in almost all of his paintings one is confronted by a miracle."

Utrillo recognized no unevenness in the quality of his production. "They are all good," he said with his engaging child-simplicity and seriousness.

He lived in Le Vesinet under Lucie's affectionate and despotic care for twenty years. In 1955 she took him south in order to avoid the chill of a Paris winter. He became ill with a sudden pulmonary congestion and died in his hotel room. He is buried in his beloved Montmartre, in the cemetery of St. Vincent, which is not more than twenty yards from the Lapin Agile.

MICHEL *The Mill of Montmartre* (74 x 102 cm) New York, Metropolitan Museum

PLATES

Utrillo and Montmartre

PLATE 1   MAURICE UTRILLO *La Butte-Pinson, Montmagny,* 1906–1907 (48 x 37 cm) Paris, Louvre

PLATE 2   Maurice Utrillo *Rue Lepic and the Moulin de la Galette*, 1908 (53 x 80 cm) Paris, Galerie Pétridès

PLATE 3   MAURICE UTRILLO *Square St. Pierre, Montmartre*, 1908 (50 x 60 cm) Paris, Galerie Pétridès

PLATE 4   MAURICE UTRILLO *La Butte-Pinson, Montmagny*, 1908 (41 x 49 cm) Saint-Tropez, Musée de l'Annonciade

PLATE 5 · MAURICE UTRILLO *Le Lapin Agile*, 1909 (50 x 65 cm) Avignon, Musée Calvet

PLATE 6 MAURICE UTRILLO *The Chaudouin House, Montmartre*, c. 1909 (46 x 61 cm) Bern, Private Collection (Photo: Mercurio)

PLATE 7   MAURICE UTRILLO *Saint-Denis,* c. 1908 (73 x 57 cm) Zurich, Kunsthaus

PLATE 8   MAURICE UTRILLO *Terrace Overlooking the Rue Muller,* 1909 (49.5 x 60.6 cm) Bern, Kunstmuseum

PLATE 9   MAURICE UTRILLO *Rue Custine*, 1909 (54 x 60 cm) Paris, Galerie Pétridès

PLATE 10 MAURICE UTRILLO *Garden at Montmagny*, c. 1909 (52 x 75 cm) Paris, Musée National d'Art Moderne

PLATE 11   MAURICE UTRILLO *Renoir's Garden at Montmartre*, 1909–10 (53 x 80 cm) New York, Collection of Grégoire Tarnopol

PLATE 12   MAURICE UTRILLO *Rue du Mont-Cenis*, 1910 (51 x 61 cm) Paris, Musée National d'Art Moderne

PLATE 13   MAURICE UTRILLO *Chartres Cathedral*, c. 1910 (92 x 65 cm) New York, Collection of Mr. and Mrs. Alex M. Lewyt

PLATE 14   MAURICE UTRILLO *Passage Cottin,* c. 1910 (62 x 46 cm) Paris, Musée National d'Art Moderne

PLATE 15   MAURICE UTRILLO *Rue Ravignan,* c. 1911 (60 x 73 cm) New York, Collection of Grégoire Tarnopol

PLATE 16 MAURICE UTRILLO *Utrillo's Arrest at Montmartre*, 1912 (37.5 x 51.5 cm) Bern, Private Collection (Photo: Howald)

PLATE 17   Maurice Utrillo *Rue Norvins*, 1912 (52.5 x 71 cm) Zurich, Kunsthaus

PLATE 18 MAURICE UTRILLO *Place du Tertre*, c. 1911–12 (50 x 73 cm) London, Tate Gallery

PLATE 19　Maurice Utrillo *14 July: Place du Tertre*, c. 1914 (45 x 60 cm) Harrison, Collection of Erna Natadon

PLATE 20   MAURICE UTRILLO *Hector Berlioz's House*, 1914 (90 x 120 cm) Paris, Louvre

PLATE 21 MAURICE UTRILLO *The Church of Nôtre-Dame de Clignancourt*, 1913–15 (73 x 100 cm) Paris, Louvre

PLATE 22   MAURICE UTRILLO *The Cathedral,* 1913 (73 x 54 cm) Paris, Louvre

PLATE 23   MAURICE UTRILLO *A la Belle Gabrielle*, c. 1914 (81 x 60 cm) Milan, Private Collection

PLATE 24 MAURICE UTRILLO *Rue du Mont-Cenis*, 1914 (72 x 100 cm) Paris, Louvre

PLATE 25 MAURICE UTRILLO *Hector Berlioz's House and Henri IV's Hunting Lodge*, c. 1917 (54 x 73 cm) Toronto, Art Gallery

PLATE 26   MAURICE UTRILLO *Woods in Montmartre*, c. 1916 (37 x 45 cm) Basel, Collection of Marcus Diener

PLATE 27   MAURICE UTRILLO *Rue des Saules,* c. 1917 (52 x 75 cm) Winterthur, Kunstmuseum

PLATE 28   MAURICE UTRILLO *Place des Abesses*, c. 1918 (65 x 99 cm) Zurich, Collection of Félix Rom

PLATE 29   MAURICE UTRILLO *Théâtre de l'Atelier, Place Dancourt, c.* 1920 (60 x 81 cm) Cologne, Wallraf-Richartz Museum

47

PLATE 30   MAURICE UTRILLO *Moulin de la Galette*, 1920 (54 x 65 cm) Paris, Private Collection

48

PLATE 31   MAURICE UTRILLO *Place du Tertre*, c. 1920 (50 x 60 cm) Zurich, Collection of Sponagel-Hirzel

PLATE 32   MAURICE UTRILLO *Rue Saint-Vincent*, c. 1918 (54 x 76 cm) Belgrade, Narodni Muzej

PLATE 33   MAURICE UTRILLO *Rue des Saules,* c. 1921 (32 x 45 cm) Paris, Private Collection

PLATE 34   MAURICE UTRILLO *Francisque Poulbot's House, Avenue Junot,* 1928 (48 x 62 cm) Paris, Galerie Pétridès

PLATE 35   MAURICE UTRILLO *Rue du Mont-Cenis*, c. 1929 (46 x 55 cm) Belgrade, Narodni Muzej

PLATE 36   MAURICE UTRILLO *Sacré-Coeur, Montmartre,* 1934 (81 x 60 cm) São Paulo, Museo de Arte

PLATE 37 MAURICE UTRILLO *Le Lapin Agile in Winter*, 1937 (51 x 81 cm) Paris, Private Collection

PLATE 38 MAURICE UTRILLO *Windmills at Montmartre*, 1948 (73 x 93.5 cm) New York, Collection of Mr. and Mrs. Harry Bakwin

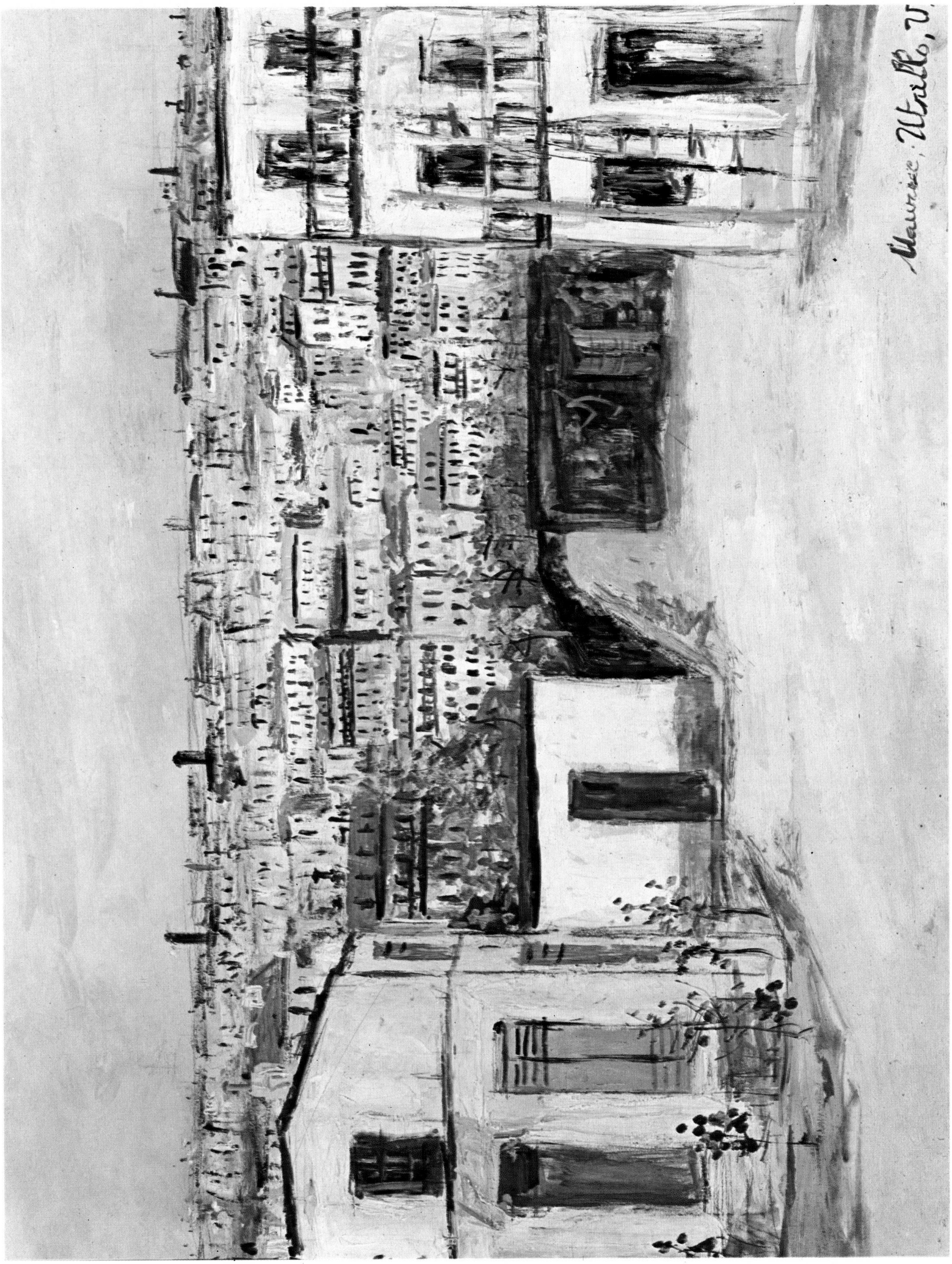

PLATE 39   Maurice Utrillo *Set Design for Act III of "Louise,"* c. 1950 (56 x 76 cm) Paris, Musée de l'Opéra

PLATE 40   MAURICE UTRILLO *Set Design for Act I of "Louise,"* c. 1950 (56 x 76 cm) Paris, Musée de l'Opéra

PLATE 41   Maurice Utrillo *Set Design for Act I of "Louise,"* c. 1950 (56 x 76 cm) Paris, Musée de l'Opéra

PLATE 42 MAURICE UTRILLO *Quai de Passy in Winter*, 1955 (180 x 300 cm) Paris, Hôtel de Ville

PLATE 43 MAURICE UTRILLO *Montmartre*, 1955 (180 x 300 cm) Paris, Hôtel de Ville

Aspects of Montmartre from Michel to Dufy

PLATE 44   GEORGES MICHEL *View of Montmartre* (18 x 30 cm) Paris, Louvre (Photo: Josse)

PLATE 45 JEAN-BAPTISTE-CAMILLE COROT *Moulin de la Galette, Montmartre*, 1840 (26 x 34 cm) Geneva, Musée d'Art et d'Histoire (Photo: J. Arland)

PLATE 46   JEAN-BAPTISTE-CAMILLE COROT *Rue Saint-Vincent*, 1850–56 (49.5 x 35 cm) Lyon, Musée des Beaux-Arts

PLATE 47   VINCENT VAN GOGH *View of Paris from Montmartre,* 1886 (38.5 x 61.5 cm) Basel, Kunstmuseum (Photo: Hinz)

PLATE 48   VINCENT VAN GOGH *Montmartre*, 1886–88 (44 x 33.5 cm) Chicago, Art Institute of Chicago, Helen Birch
Bartlett Memorial Collection

PLATE 49   ALPHONSE QUIZET *Rue des Saules,* c. 1910 (94 x 76 cm) Paris, Musée d'Art Moderne de la Ville

PLATE 50 EDGAR DEGAS *Women in Front of a Cafe, Evening,* 1877 (42 x 60 cm) Paris, Louvre

PLATE 51 · Henri de Toulouse-Lautrec *Woman Drinking (Suzanne Valadon)*, 1889 (48 x 65 cm) Albi, Musée Toulouse-Lautrec

PLATE 52   ALEXANDRE STEINLEN *Chansons de Montmartre*, c. 1899, Paris, Bibliothèque Nationale

PLATE 53   ALEXANDRE STEINLEN *The Lunch Hour*, Paris, Bibliothèque Nationale

PLATE 54   ALEXANDRE STEINLEN *Bal de La Barrière*, 1898, Paris, Bibliothèque Nationale

PLATE 55   PIERRE BONNARD *Les Grands Boulevards*, 1898 (26 x 33 cm) London, Collection of R. J. Sainsbury

PLATE 56   GIOVANNI BOLDINI *Leaving the Masked Ball at Montmartre*, 1875 (32.5 x 46 cm) Pistoia, Private Collection

PLATE 57   GINO SEVERINI *Avenue Trudaine, Sweet Stall,* 1908 (59 x 72 cm) Paris, Private Collection

PLATE 58   JUAN GRIS *Still Life Before an Open Window: Place Ravignan*, 1915 (116 x 89 cm) Philadelphia, Museum of
Art, Arensberg Collection

PLATE 59   RAOUL DUFY *The Artist's Studio, Impasse of Guelma near Place Pigalle*, 1939 (119 x 148 cm) Paris, Bérès Collection

PLATE 60   SUZANNE VALADON *Self-Portrait*, 1883 (45 x 31 cm) Paris, Musée National d'Art Moderne

THE ARTISTS

BONNARD *House in the Court*, 1895, Paris, Bibliothèque Nationale

GIOVANNI BOLDINI

Born in Ferrara, December 31, 1842, the eighth of thirteen brothers. He attended the university, but he was mainly interested in the paintings and frescos of the great masters. In 1863 he moved to Florence, where he visited galleries and museums and attended, in the evenings, the famous academy for the study of painting. Later he rented a studio and assumed the life of an artist, while at the same time moving in the best society.

On his first visit to Paris in 1867 for the World's Fair, he was amazed at the people, the life, and the extraordinary personalities of that city. He returned to Florence and worked incessantly, painting portraits and studying. In the fall of 1870, at the invitation of Sir Conwallis-West, whom he had met in Florence, he went to London to paint portraits of his family. Boldini soon became very successful, and the most famous people in London posed for him. In spite of this, he still remembered his visit to Paris, and in 1871 he decided to return there, intending to go back to Italy as soon as he had achieved a certain reputation. Instead he remained there the remainder of his life. He delighted in painting young and beautiful women, not professional models, in quick and spontaneous poses, and he painted with humor and keen observation the countless phases of gay and boisterous life in Montmartre. In a short time Boldini became popular among Parisian artists, dealers acquired his canvases, and his studio in Place Pigalle became the meeting place for new friends, from the revolutionary marquis Henri Rochefort to Degas, Lautrec, and the Goncourt brothers. In 1875 he won success at the Salon d'Automne. In 1886 he moved to a small villa in Boulevard

Berthier; through that studio passed celebrities from all over the world and the most beautiful of the music-hall artists.

Boldini traveled to New York, where an exhibit of his work took place in November, 1897. On October 19, 1929, he married an Italian journalist. He died on January 31, 1931.

PIERRE BONNARD

Born on October 30, 1867, in Fontenay-aux-Roses. His father persuaded him to study law, which he continued with until he had obtained his law degree. Continuing his studies further, he also frequented the Julian Academy and met Vuillard, Maurice Denis, Roussel, and Vallaton. He competed unsuccessfully for the Prix de Rome and continued to work without allowing this dis-

BONNARD *Street Corner Seen from Above*, 1895, Paris, Bibliothèque Nationale

appointment to affect him. He visited museums and discovered an interest in Chinese and Japanese art.

Bonnard was one of the first adherents of the Nabis group; he quickly divested himself of influences and theories and soon found himself part of the group of the *Revue Blanche,* of which he was one of the founders and for which he made numerous illustrations. In 1889 he decided definitely to devote his time to painting. Two years later he exhibited at the Salon des Indépendents, where the critic Gustave Geffroy commented on his entries. In 1896 Bonnard had an important exhibit at Vollard's. Although he was appreciated for "his marvelous ability as a painter in gray and dark tones," he nevertheless changed his palette. His vision of the world brightened, and he continued to analyze with deep penetration the light that animated and illumined people and objects. When he exhibited at Bernheim's in 1904, he showed a series of canvases, studies of

VALADON *Self-Portrait,* 1903, Paris, Musée National d'Art Moderne

of the group of the "Jeune Peinture Française," all the museums of the world sought to acquire his canvases. Bonnard kept himself apart from the bustle and conflict of the times. After the death of his wife in 1942, he retired to "Le Cannet," where he led a quiet life, entirely devoted to painting, until his death on January 23, 1947.

JEAN-BAPTISTE-CAMILLE COROT

Born in Paris in 1796 of well-to-do parents. After working briefly with a clothes merchant, he devoted himself, after 1822, exclusively to painting. He studied with the landscapist Michallon and the Academician Bertin, and, in Fontainebleau, on the outskirts of Paris and also along the Channel coast, he practiced analytical drawing from nature, according to classic rules.

His first visit to Italy, from 1825 to 1827, was essential for his experience of classic tradition and Mediterranean light, which gave to his scenes of Rome and other places in Italy a new clarity and simplicity. Upon returning to France he established a working method that was taken as a model by the young generation of landscapists: in winter he made large studio compositions for the Salon, which followed the attention of Lorrain and Poussin, and in the summer he painted outdoors, traveling throughout France. He made his debut at the Salon of 1831 with four landscapes; in 1833 he won the gold medal second-class, and after 1840 he won governmental commissions and, in 1846, the medal of the Legion of Honor. Except for a third visit to Italy in 1843 and brief trips to Holland in 1854 and to London in 1862, he lived all his life in France, and worked in the outskirts of Paris and on the family estate in Ville d'Avray. He was acquainted with Millet, Rousseau, Troyon, Diaz, and Dupré, and particularly friendly with Daubigny. After 1852 they worked and traveled together in Morvan.

VALADON *Portrait of Miguel Utrillo,* 1891

female figures that were vibrant with delicate color harmonies. His predilection for effects of light impelled him to divide his time between "Le Cannet," in winter, and Normandy. In 1920 he achieved a fusion of light, color, and drawing.

Bonnard's prestige was great, and after 1918, when he was made, along with Renoir, president

Many young landscape artists derived their method from Corot; his simple landscape studies from real life influenced the direct observation of nature of the Impressionists. He died in Ville d'Avray on February 22, 1875.

EDGAR HILAIRE DEGAS

Born in Paris on July 19, 1834, son of the wealthy banker Auguste de Gas. After finishing his secondary studies and serving a brief apprenticeship in the studio of the painter Barrias, he enrolled in the courses of Henri Lamothe, a disciple of Ingres. A year later he decided to take courses at the Fine Arts Academy.

In 1854 he visited Naples and in 1856 he returned to Italy, stopping in Florence at the home of

VALADON *Portrait of Maurice Utrillo*, 1910

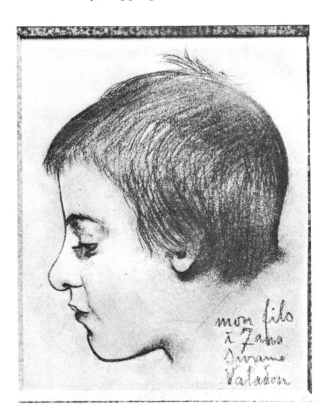

VALADON *Portrait of Maurice Utrillo at the Age of Seven*, 1890, Paris, Galerie Pétridès

his uncle Baron Bellelli. He was in Italy again in 1858, stopping in Rome, Viterbo, Orvieto (where he admired and copied the frescos of Signorelli), Perugia, Assisi, and Florence, where he was again the guest of his uncle and began the painting *The Bellelli Family*. Between 1860 and 1865, under the influence of Ingres and the Italian masters, he devoted himself to historical and mythological subjects. Around 1865, following his meeting with Manet and the group of artists of the Cafe Guerbois, his interests changed and he turned to contemporary life for his painting subjects.

In 1872 Degas became interested in the milieu of the opera, introduced there by a member of the orchestra, Desiré Dihau. After a trip to America, to New Orleans, he took part in the first Impressionist exhibition in 1874, entering ten paintings.

In 1881 he produced his first sculpture in wax. He continued to be active during his later years although his eyesight began to weaken. In 1886 he exhibited a series of ten nudes in pastel at the eighth and last Impressionist show. Before 1890 he made several more journeys, to Italy, Spain, and Morocco. Then he withdrew from society more and more. He died in Paris on September 27, 1917.

RAOUL DUFY

Born in Le Havre, June 3, 1877. At fourteen he went to work, but he attended evening courses in fine arts at the Municipal School of Le Havre. Among his fellow students were Friesz and Braque. In 1899 he received a scholarship to the School of Fine Arts in Paris, where, with Friesz, he enrolled at the studio of Leon Bonnat.

In 1901 he exhibited at the Salon des Artistes Français, in 1903 at the Salon des Indépendants, and in 1905 at the Salon d'Automne. His first one-man show was at the Berthe Weill Gallery in 1906. After 1904 he was in contact with the Fauves and was greatly influenced by Matisse. In 1907 and 1908 his painting took on a Cubist formulation; his palette became severe, almost monochromatic. He also designed textiles for Paul Poiret and did a series of engravings for the *Bestiary* of Guillaume Apollinaire. In 1914 he was drafted into the army. In 1920 he settled in Vence, France, where he did a series of landscapes that he exhibited at Bernheim-Jeune. Besides painting in oil and watercolor he made designs for textiles and wallpaper and worked in ceramics and wood engraving. He visited Taormina in 1922 and Morocco in 1926 with Poiret. These journeys decisively influenced his painting of those years, which is characterized by

UTTER *Portrait of Maurice Utrillo*, 1910

an extensive luminosity and brilliant colors. In 1925 he took part in the International Exposition of Decorative Arts in Paris, and in 1930 he made the sets for the ballet *Palm Beach*. He also illustrated several books. For the Paris World's Fair of 1937, he painted a large panel, sixty by ten meters, entitled *Electricity*.

He lived in several different cities in France. Later, suffering from polyarthritis, he settled in Perpignan, where he was treated by a doctor-friend. In 1947 he had a large one-man show at the Louis Carré Gallery in Paris. In 1950 he visited the United States and exhibited at two shows in New York. At the Venice Biennial of 1952, he won the International Prize for painting. Dufy died March 23, 1963, in Forcalquier.

JUAN GRIS

José Victoriano Gonzales, who later took the name of Juan Gris, was born in Madrid on March 23, 1887. As a very young man he worked as illustrator on the magazines *Blanco y Negro* and *Madrid Comico*, and in 1904 he enrolled in a painting course with José Maria Carbonero, after studying at the School of Arts and Crafts in Madrid. In 1906 he arrived in Paris and soon became part of the group that frequented Picasso's studio. Meanwhile he worked for several magazines, *L'Assiette au Beurre*, *Le Charivari*, and *Le Témoin*, and in 1908 he met the art dealer Kahnweiler, with whom he signed a contract a few years later.

In 1911 he painted his first Cubist picture. The following year he exhibited a portrait of Picasso in the Salon des Indépendents, and he also exhibited in the Section d'Or. At this time he met Josette, the woman with whom he was to spend the rest of his life. In 1913 he spent the summer working with Picasso at Ceret in the eastern Pyrenees, and during the following winter he devoted himself to experiments with papiers collés.

During World War I, Kahnweiler took refuge in Switzerland, and Gris found himself in ever increasing financial difficulties. He alleviated his financial problems in 1916 by selling all of his productions to Léonce Rosenberg and was thus able to spend the rest of the war years in Tourraine. In 1919 he had his first large one-man show at L'Effort Moderne of Rosenberg. In 1922 he made his home in Boulogne-sur-Seine. He exhibited in Paris and abroad, produced etchings and lithographs, but suffered from declining health. He died in Boulogne-sur-Seine on May 11, 1927.

GEORGES MICHEL

Born in Paris on January 12, 1763, to a poor family. At twelve he entered the studio of the historical painter Leduc, but, because of his interest in the study of nature, he soon began painting landscapes of Paris and its surroundings. He married while very young, and at the age of twenty he already had five children. In 1785 he journeyed down the Rhine to Switzerland, and there he formed a friendship with the celebrated Elizabeth Vigée-Lebrun that lasted all his life.

With his friend and companion Lazare Bruandet, Michel wandered through the forests around Paris, Boulogne, and Barbizon, his sketchbook in hand. He was especially fond of the Montmartre windmills that he painted several times. He also worked at the restoration of Flemish and Dutch paintings for the Louvre. At the death of his wife in 1827, he became very withdrawn, living a life apart from others and devoting himself entirely to painting. At this time Baron d'Ivry, who held Michel in great esteem, supported him and gave him a pension on the condition that the artist work for him. At the end of 1830, the Louvre acquired one of Michel's works. The artist, considered one of the forerunners of the modern French landscapists, continued his sequestered life until his death on June 17, 1843, in Paris.

ALPHONSE QUIZET

Born in Paris on March 13, 1885. His father was a brigadier in the Municipal Guard. Quizet was a good student, especially in drawing and geometry. He was given a scholarship to the École Colbert, a secondary school, but he wanted very much to become a painter. One day in 1903 as he was painting in the rue Cortot at the top of the Butte, he met

Maurice Utrillo. They formed a close friendship and often painted together. Quizet worked for some time in the studio of the architects Brunel and Potier, obtaining fine experience there. In 1914 he joined the army and was commissioned to draw up a plan for heavy artillery. During the war the Salon des Artistes Français opened its doors to artists serving in the armed forces, and Quizet sent his first work, *Rue des Saules*, which was immediately accepted. He took part in the Salon des Indépendents in 1922.

Quizet came to be known as "the painter of the Faubourgs." He was fascinated by the suburbs of Paris, which he probed with his brilliant palette, discovering an ingenuous poetry in the changing morning and evening light on crumbling facades and on barren walls. He died in Paris in 1955.

GINO SEVERINI

Born in Cortona on April 7, 1883. He was brought up by his grandparents and even as a boy showed a passionate interest for painting. For this reason he went to Rome in 1899 and shared a despicable

QUIZET *View of Paris from Montmartre*, 1910, Geneva, Petit Palais

attic room with his mother. To combat this poverty he resigned himself to the most menial work. He met other young people who were becoming interested in social problems, and, at this time, he read Marx, Hegel, and Nietzsche.

With Boccioni, whom he met in 1900, he painted along the Tiber and in the environs of Rome. He met Giacomo Balla too, who instructed him in the Divisionist technique.

In 1904 he exhibited for the first time in Rome an Impressionist painting that was favorably received by the critics. In 1906 he moved to Paris,

UTRILLO *The House of Mimi Pinson*, c. 1920, Paris, Collection of André Morisset

where he became friendly with another Italian artist who lived in rue Lepic, Amedeo Modigliani.

The gentle, modest, shy Severini became a revolutionary ready to dare anything, and in 1910 he abandoned painting to become a pilot. However, he had a change of heart and returned, without a penny, ready to begin all over again.

With Boccioni, Carra, and Russolo he signed, on February 11, 1910, the Futurist Manifesto, which opposed imitation of the past. The meetings with Guillaume Apollinaire, Pierre Reverdy, and Paul Fort gave him the opportunity to broaden his culture and to become acquainted with the intellectual life of Paris. He also met Picasso, with whom he met frequently to discuss painting problems. On April 7, 1913, Severini had a show at the Marlborough Gallery in London, which received great acclaim in the press. On August 28 he married Jeanne Fort, the daughter of Paul Fort.

In the autumn of 1916 Modigliani introduced him to the art dealer Léonce Rosenberg, who arranged a verbal contract with him for "the right to a first look" at all of his works.

At the end of the war he made several mosaic decorations and frescos in palaces and churches (the castle of Montefugoni near Florence, the church of Notre Dame du Valentin in Lausanne). In 1933 he did mosaics for the Triennale in Milan. He also illustrated several books: *L'Amour, enfant de Bohème* by Paul Fort, *Fleurs et masques* and *El Cementario marino* by Paul Valéry.

In 1935 he received first prize in painting at the Quadriennale in Rome. He exhibited in Milan, in Rome in 1942, and in Paris, always with success, and continued to work on easel paintings, mosaics, and frescos.

The continual exhibits, in New York in 1954, at the San Paolo Biennale in 1957 in Rome, at the Biennale in Venice in 1960, brought worldwide acquaintance with Severini's work. He died in Paris, February 26, 1966. On June 11, 1967, a large retrospective show of his most representative work was held at the National Museum of Modern Art in Paris.

ALEXANDRE STEINLEN

Born in Lausanne in 1859. His father was a teacher of drawing, and Steinlen drew and sketched a great deal, especially cats. At twenty he went to Mulhouse, where he studied decorative drawing; like his compatriot Eugene Grasset, Steinlen made designs for fabrics. In 1881 he arrived in Paris, where he met Aristide Bruant and, to earn a living, made his debut at Le Chat Noir, managed by Rodolphe Salis. In 1891 a large daily paper launched a literary supplement, the *Gil Blas Illustré;* every issue contained a large drawing in color by Steinlen, who made his reputation with this publication. In Montmartre he became friendly with Gérault-Richard, a young socialist full of revolutionary ardor, who founded *Le Chambard Socialiste,* in which he denounced social inequities and government corruption. Steinlen collaborated with him, completely at home in this

VALADON *Portrait of Maurice Utrillo*, Private Collection

STEINLEN *"Montmartre, Suite de Valses,"* 1897, Paris, Bibliothèque Nationale

element, giving the full measure of his talent and of his courage. He was a talented, painstaking artist; his drawings and posters brought him a modest living. His illustrations gave him the opportunity to deride the blind egoism and ineptitude of a bourgeois society that was already dead; his best pictures, however, are those in which he represents the poverty and suffering of the lower classes. A deep thinker and critic, his sensitivity and understanding enabled him to observe and to assimilate what went on around him.

After a life of passionate dedication to his work, Steinlen died in Paris at the age of sixty-four.

MAURICE UTRILLO

Born December 26, 1883, son of Marie-Clémentine Valadon, who would later be known as the painter Suzanne Valadon.

On January 27, 1891, Maurice was adopted by the journalist and art critic Miguel Utrillo, a friend of Suzanne and of Paul Moussis. Suzanne and Moussis later were married and moved to a small villa near Montmagny. At thirteen Maurice attended the College Rollin in Paris as a day student; after classes, before returning home, he regularly stopped at the Cafe des Oiseaux to drink.

In 1901 the first psychic disorders became apparent in his outbursts of rage under the influence of alcohol; he was confined in the Institute of Ste. Anne, where Dr. Vallon treated him for alcoholism. After two months he was recovering in Montmagny, and his mother attempted to interest him in painting, for which he showed no

enthusiasm at first. In 1904 he returned to Montmartre, to rue Cortot, and sold his paintings for drinking money—the studies from that period, almost always signed Maurice Valadon, were scattered about in disreputable taverns. His mother, who broke with Moussis in 1909, lived in the Impasse de Guelma at that time and was often awakened by the police because of disturbances such as fights and the breaking of windows caused by Maurice when drunk.

That very year, however, Utrillo's work became

UTRILLO *Le Lapin Agile*, c. 1916, Collection of A. Manteau

UTRILLO *Moulin de la Galette*, 1924, Perpignan, Collection of Belzeaux

more intense, and characteristic colors appeared with a preponderance of white; he sold to dealers and collectors and exhibited at the Salon d'Automne.

In the spring of 1912 he was confined in Sannois in the care of Dr. Revertegat. The following year, from May 26 to June 9, Libaude exhibited thirty-one of Utrillo's paintings, and the same year Utrillo exhibited three paintings at the Salon des Indépendents. In 1916 he was placed in an institution in Villejuif and released in November. Zborowski supported him with a small income.

In 1916 he was treated by Dr. Vicq, in the clinic in Aulnay-sous-Bois; after six months he escaped and returned to the cafe Casse-Croute, but before the end of the year he voluntarily went for treatment to Dr. Briand at the clinic in Picpus.

In 1919 at the Lepoultre Gallery his work from 1910 to 1915 was exhibited with considerable success. Utrillo escaped from the clinic in Picpus and the authorities ordered him to be kept under the constant surveillance of a male nurse, Pierre. After 1921 he had several shows at the Berthe Weill Gallery and at Bernheim-Jeune, and he took part in the Salon d'Automne. The artist, who was by this time famous, returned to rue Cortot. In 1924, after attempting suicide by trying to break his head against the wall of the police station, he spent a long period of convalescence in Ain at the chateau of Saint-Bernard that he, his mother, and her new husband, Utter, had acquired.

In May of 1926 the "Barabau" company of Sergei Diaghilev performed a ballet by Balanchine with

UTRILLO *View of Montmartre*, c. 1933

sets and costumes designed by Utrillo. During these years the artist's new style developed, in which the tragic element disappeared and colors became strong and violent. In 1935 he married Lucie Valore and retired to his villa in Le Vesinet, where, under the constant, loving surveillance of his wife, he drank modestly and painted a great deal. In 1942 a large exhibit of his work took place at the Galerie Pétridès. He died November 16, 1955.

SUZANNE VALADON

Born in a village in the vicinity of Limoges in 1867. Her real name was Marie-Clémentine. Having no family, she moved to Paris, where she earned her living with work of the humblest kind: she sold vegetables in the market of les Halles, waited on tables in cheap taverns, accompanied the children of wealthy parents to les Tuileries. Then she changed her name to Suzanne, moved to Montmartre, and became a model; she posed for Puvis de Chavannes and Renoir and met Degas, who became her friend and took an interest in the events of her life. She also frequented the studio of Toulouse-Lautrec, who appreciated her and admired her drawings. Ambroise Vollard and other dealers bought her drawings. In 1883, at the age of sixteen, she gave birth to a son, Maurice, who would later be recognized by Miguel Utrillo, a Spanish journalist. In 1896 Suzanne married Paul Moussis, and her life became more tranquil. The family moved to a small villa in Montmagny.

Maurice attended the College Rollin and, in commuting between school and home, he began to drink. Suzanne was able to devote herself more actively to drawing and painting; the hard facts of her life had accustomed her to viewing men and events with implacable realism. She alternated nude studies with portraits in crayon, oils, and pastels. In 1909 she divorced Paul Moussis and two years later married the young painter André Utter, and occupied a studio in rue Cortot. Suzanne was also a wonderful mother, always ready to run to the aid of her son, a genial but vagabond artist and an alcoholic who was often arrested for disturbances and accidents. In 1912 she exhibited at the Levy Gallery and the Berthe Weill Gallery with excellent critical reviews. In 1923 Suzanne Valadon, with Utter and Utrillo, acquired the chateau Saint-Bernard in Ain, where the three artists spent the best seasons of the year painting together.

Three years later they moved to a villa in Avenue Junot, where Utrillo, finally recovered,

UTRILLO *Théâtre de l'Atelier*, 1924, Perpignan, Collection of Georges Belzeaux

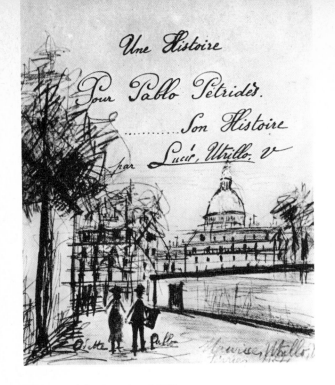

UTRILLO *Montmartre*, 1937

worked very seriously, helped by his mother and Utter, with whom he formed a close friendship.

As time passed the group became more stormy. Utter decided to move to the studio in rue Cortot, while Suzanne and Maurice remained in Avenue Junot, where they continued their pleasant life working together. In 1935 Maurice married Lucie Valore, and Suzanne was left alone. She died in Paris on April 7, 1938.

VINCENT VAN GOGH

Born March 30, 1853, at Groot Zundert in Dutch Brabant. His father started him on his career as an art dealer. He worked at the branch office of the Goupil Gallery in the Hague, then in the London office, and finally in the main gallery in Paris. A passionate lover of painting, he suddenly left his employment at the beginning of 1876, but he did not yet know what he wanted to pursue. He read a great deal, drew a great deal, and was often seized with religious furor. He became a language teacher at Ramsgate in Kent, then an assistant preacher in Isleworth near London, next a bookseller in Dordrecht, theology student in Amsterdam, and student in Brussels in courses in preaching. In January of 1879, Van Gogh obtained the position of lay preacher among the miners of the Borinage, where he shared the toils and privations of the miners. Here in the Borinage he realized his true vocation after a profound examination of conscience in the summer of 1880, and from here he departed with an exhaustion from which he never recovered.

After leaving the Borinage, Van Gogh moved first to Brussels, where he studied anatomy and

perspective, and then to Etten. In 1881 at the Hague, he began painting. After a stay in Nuenen and Anvers, he joined his brother Theo in Paris. There he attended Cormon's classes and met Toulouse-Lautrec and Anquetin, took part in the lively discussions that followed the Impressionist crisis, sided with the Divisionists and Synthetists, and met such artists as Pissarro, Seurat, Signac, Bernard, and Gauguin. With the latter he formed his strongest friendship and when he returned to Arles to work, Gauguin joined him on October 20, 1888. Together they worked actively, but the difference in their temperaments and their constant arguments frayed the delicate nerves of Van Gogh. On the evening of December 23, armed with a razor, he tried to attack his friend. Shortly after, to punish himself, he turned

UTRILLO *Sacré-Coeur*, c. 1935

his weapon against himself and cut off his ear. This was the first of the crises that disturbed his last years. In May of 1889 he entered the psychiatric hospital of San Remy in Provence to undergo rigorous treatment. A year later he moved to Auvers-sur-Oise, where Dr. Gachet treated him. All seemed to be going well, but two months later, on a day when his mind was affected with hallucinations, he shot himself through the heart in the open country. Two days later, on July 29, 1890, he died in the presence of his beloved brother Theo and his friend Dr. Gachet.

List of Illustrations